The Six o'clock Siren

A personal journey through breast cancer

Sandra Evans Falconer

~ And To Jane —
My
~ These poems
Bring you Comfort —
In love & Sisterhood
Sandra Evans Falconer

Otter Bay Books
BALTIMORE, MD 2009

Front Cover photo by Lori Neikirk

Please direct all correspondence and book orders to:
Sandra Evans Falconer
evansfalconer@aol.com

Library of Congress Control Number 2009937863
ISBN 978-0-578-03905-3

Published for the author by
Otter Bay Books
3507 Newland Road
Baltimore, MD 21218-2513

Printed in the United States of America

For
Gregory M. Hall, MD
and
Paul B. Fowler, MD
who saved my life

My thanks to the following publications in which some of these poems first appeared:

The Oncologist: "Next Week," "Recovery," "Her Treatment Begins," "After Breast Cancer," "Good Report," and "Years Out."

Coping With Cancer: "Solids," "Guide Book," "Blue Bike."

Perpetumm Mobile: "Wonder Women," "Women Inventors"

Ars Medica: "On the Gurney with the Village People"

Reed: "September Morning"

The poem *"Sewing Patterns"* won the 2nd place award in the 2008 Poetry Contest for *The Baltimore Review.*

Contents

SECTION ONE: *A Very Random Snow* 1

Acela Express 2

January Absolutes 4

Sewing Patterns 6

Skein of Things 8

Litanies 10

Wonder Woman 12

Why I want to look like Everyone Else Today 14

On the Gurney with the Village People 16

Recovery 18

Night Prayers 20

SECTION TWO: *First Day of Gorgeous Weather* 23

Brownies 24

Her Treatment Begins 26

Shine the Light on Me 28

The Woman Who Lived 30

"C" 32

Solids 34

Biafine 36

Restoration... 38

Women Inventors 40

After Breast Cancer.................................... 42

A Good Report... 44

SECTION THREE: *Living in the Spring*............... 47

Blue Bike 48

Guide Book.. 50

Poem.. 52

Jupiter 54

Blossoms... 56

September Morning 58

Years Out 59

Lifeboats... 60

Going Easy 62

Party, April 2004.. 64

About the Author.. 67

From the Author

When I was first diagnosed with cancer, people said to me: *having cancer is like going through a new door.* I found this a strange but deeply true statement. Three weeks after my second surgery, I began the MFA In Writing Program at Spalding University in Louisville, Kentucky. Over the course of my incredible two years at Spalding, I wrote all the poems which appear in this book, and did so with the help and support of many people. To my writing mentors, who saw these poems come alive, I am very grateful: Greg Pape, a "good shepherd" to the early poems and the person who taught me most about metaphor; to Jeanie Thompson, who helped me weave a compelling sequence of work; to Kathleen Driskell, who showed me my inner "Warrior Queen," and also helped me learn to listen so carefully to each poem's unique voice and need; and to Rane Arroyo, who edited this manuscript and made its music and power that much more beautiful – to all these poets and teachers and guides who believed in the poet in me, I feel very grateful.

To Molly Peacock, who helped me ferry these poems to a place of illumination and meaning, and to Richard Cecil, who showed me how humor saves and confounds even the bleakest places, I give great thanks. Both served as my workshop leaders and took these poems through their paces, saw them through various incarnations, and always believed in them.

I thank the Spalding writing community who came and sat with me on various shores on sunny and cloudy days both, while we wrote and re-wrote and wrote again, scribbled fast when the Muse spoke or whispered, steeled ourselves, or put the critical bug to rest, listened, waited, worked, and created a piece of writing that both surprised and saved us, and finally congratulated ourselves for being brave enough to be writers. To all my workshop cohorts, thesis committee members, those who heard my work over the years, all those kindred spirits who sat in the elegant lobby of the Brown Hotel and held forth on as many and varied topics as human beings can hold forth on, I am also grateful. I especially want to thank Susan Gilliam for her support and care and spectacular sense of humor which always gets me going; Cynthia Allar, who patiently sent these poems and this book out into the world so many times; Frances Nicholson, whose intelligence and strength have been a light for me, and Dawn Shamp, who kept me in the writing life and showed me the gallant beauty of a yellow fan.

In addition to my writing life, I thank Artemis, my dance muse, my teacher, and friend. Through dance and music, through deep wisdom and the Goddess energy, she showed me how to use the power of the dance for my own personal narrative. I have danced for breast cancer survivors, my mother and her friends, nursing home residents, assisted living programs, and senior centers. The dance and all its expressions in veils and fans continue to be a flowing wellspring of health and healing in my life.

To my Arm in Arm support group sisters: Ellen, Jo, Katherine, Florence, Pat, Stephanie, Marcette and Linola – every one of them spirited and caring, wise and funny, spunky, and triumphant. They're all champions. I thank also the women of the Pink Ribbon Poetry Group in Vorhees, New Jersey, who asked me to speak and attend one of their writing sessions. The poems I heard one evening in October of 2004 were simply heart breaking, defiant, hilarious, and ultimately victorious.

I am honored to thank Alison Evans of the Baltimore chapter of The American Cancer Society who asked me to read at several Baltimore events. She has cheered me on every time.

And I thank so many good and loving friends, beginning with Lucy Mauro, who stood by my side through the diagnosis, surgery, and radiation. She is a wonderful and treasured gift in my life. And she is the *Lucy* who appears in many of these poems. Also, Lori Neikirk, who sang disco with me in the car on the way to my second surgery, brings a joy to my life that is immeasurable. And Melissa Perry, my voice teacher, who showed me not only my true "voice," but who has been such a kind, inspirational, and generous friend. Many other friends, whose care and concern has lifted me, join them: Wendy Shuford, David Smith, Jill Arold, Liz Neely, Jim Meyer, Bill Krim, Keith Parker, Linda Sillin, Lexi Bishopwhite, Marcia Smith, and Sherry Morgan, to name but a few. I am truly touched by the care of my two aunts, Mary Bell and Marney Sherman, who have been my champions for so long. And for my brother Peter, who knows my various accoutrements and asked Lucy if I'd worn eye shadow the day of my surgery. I am very thankful for the support of The Light Street Presbyterian Church, and for the special care from Mother Bethel Church in Philadelphia as well.

And for a dear friend who is absent now – Laurie Stedman, my closest bond, who lost her 15 year battle with breast cancer in March of 2009 – I pray the light of these poems will find you and hold you and keep you. You who called me "my sister," and who sang the "King of Spain" with me in the car all the way up to Mother Bethel and back again – you will always be in my heart.

To my mother most of all, who put off her chores to read me stories about tigers turning to butter and magical pumpkins. She, too, is a survivor of 38 years. Now in her 87th year, she continues to live her life with hope and grace and spirit. She is also quite proud – and rightly so – to have the best line in this book (see the poem, "Restoration.")

To my Muse, who has been with me since the beginning, and who makes all the magic happen.

And to my sisters, whoever you are, I say: May God keep us as we go. Carry on, my sisters, Carry on!

Sandra Evans Falconer
Baltimore, Maryland
August, 2009

I am my own heroine

> Marie Bashkirtseff, (1874) *Journal* (1887)

The goal is to live a full, productive life even with all that ambiguity. No matter what happens, whether the cancer never flares up again or whether you die, the important thing is that the days that you have had, you will have *lived*.

> Gilda Radner, *It's Always Something* (1989)

Section One

A Very Random Snow

Acela Express

I was sitting in the recovery room's
small green flowered chair,
sipping a cup of hot coffee,
and dressed again in my pink silk slacks,
jersey top, and black wool jacket,
my big leather bag beside me.

*You looked like you were waiting
for the Acela,* Lucy said one day,
remembering the time
she picked me up after surgery.

I heard her and the voices
of patients and their families.
I watched the thin curve of steam rising
from the coffee pot,
and the faint, steady, *beep, beep
beep* of the bedside monitors.

Neither Lucy or I talked about
the thick white bandage across my chest,
or how I'd need to prop a pillow
under my side to sleep,
or how I'd cry the next day
tossing a toy mouse for Degas.

Lucy was right: I was like someone
waiting in a crowded train station,
checking my watch, ready to pick up
my bag, step aboard, vanish,
leave everything behind.

The surgery was over. But whenever
I looked out the train window,
I'd see it there,
over and over again.

January Absolutes

Something's not right
with this latest mammogram.
The radiologist next to me points
to a large whitish area

in the center of the film.
I've had a mass here,
unpleasant but harmless
for three decades now, only

this January it looks different:
bigger, wider, colder,
a swollen sac flecked
with way too much white,

pushing against the edges
as if whatever's inside
there is after me.
I lean forward,
my back arched
away from the metal chair.

The radiologist is talking
her words fading, or
her voice too distant
for me to hear.

All I want now is the world
to speak in absolutes:
Yes/No, black/White.
This isn't my film.

And this new thing I stare at
whatever it is, is wrong,
wrong turn, wrong map,

it's absolutely wrong.

Sewing Patterns

The worst part about the biopsy
wasn't the injection –

it was the way the needle
removed those few swirling cells.
The sound reminded me
of a sewing machine,
drilling its way
along the outer edge of my breast.

And sewing is not a good image for me:
it takes me back to Junior High School -
a D in Home Ec class.
Even when the other girls showed me,
I couldn't thread the bobbin.

I cut as close as I could to the pattern
on the smooth brown paper
but I wasn't close enough –
bad edges, my teacher said.

By mistake, I cut off an apron tie,
then flunked the final.

Even now, forty years later,
if I walk into a craft shop
and happen to see those dress patterns
piled up along the racks,
I turn away,

I see the ghosts of shirtwaists
botched back in Home Ec class

where despite my uneven buttonholes,
and my lopsided stitches,
I just wanted to know
everything would be all right.

Skein of Things

These cells, Lucy says,
and I know she's talking about the biopsy —
aren't about you.

They're not part of your life,
my nurse friend David tells me.
It's true.

They've nothing to do with the way
I talk to Degas when he cries
until I put his treats down,

or the dinner parties I have
where my friends and I sit
around the old trunk by the fireplace,

or even how I practice the scales, e, a, ah,
late at night
when none of my neighbors are up.

These cells don't belong
to you, Lucy says,
and I imagine her flinging them

hard and fast and far away,
the cells I have but don't want
in the life I'm living now,

friends on the phone,
Degas carefully cleaning his
small yellow dish,

the e's and ah's I'm sending from my one body
the same scales, my favorites, the ones I'm practicing
all this week, and the next.

Litanies

Today, after the worried radiologist
told me the results of my biopsy –
this is not the outcome we wanted

and, stress is always a factor -
I walked home, sat at my desk,
and wrote the following:

When I wasn't hired
for the job at the rehab hospital,
a job I thought I'd do well in,

when I gained ten pounds
the year after menopause,
and couldn't get into my suits,

when I didn't visit Steven at Worthington
after he called me at my dorm
to say the staff took away his belt

When I lived on Clinton Street
and thought I might cut both my wrists
and lie down in the long white bathtub,

When Richard went in for shock treatments,
When Dylan died at Fellowship House
When Nina died and they called me at work

When my father disappeared.
When I heard on the news that Ginger had died
When Dennis killed himself.

At the top of this page
I've written, March 2003,
the year it snowed randomly

all over Maryland, much more
than anyone expected it to.
The year when inside the cells

of my own body, something –
something happened, and all I
could do was write the word, *when*.

Wonder Woman

Wednesday night and I'm making
strawberry Jell-O
to have tomorrow

when I come home from the hospital
after the surgery.

What are you doing? Lucy asks
when she calls earlier.

Making Jell-O, I say, bringing
the phone into the kitchen,

where I stand
with the one surprisingly solid

small box,
a giant strawberry on the front.

I mix the red powder with water,
pour it into the glass dishes on the counter.

I try to tell Lucy how I feel:

Whenever I make this,
I feel like the heroine
of my own story:

Plucky Girl, Warrior Queen,
the one you always put your hopes on.

I love it, Lucy says*:*
How's the Jell-O?

A little less shaky, I tell her.

Why I want to Look like Everyone Else Today

It's nine o'clock in the morning.
I'm at the hospital,
taking my clothes off
in the empty dressing room
down the hall from Breast Localizations.
I'm wearing the regulation footies.
Now I'm onto the gown –
gowns actually,
one for the front,
one for the back.
In between are two rows of metal snaps.
Ten minutes in the dressing room,
and I still can't get my left arm
into my left sleeve.

Right now,
I want to look like everyone else:
the staff in their wool blazers
pressed pantsuits, and nice scarfs,
walking in for morning rounds.
Instead, I'm about to be wheeled
through two doors that go *whoosh,*
where someone will cover me
with blue drapes,
and open up my one human body
dressed in a gown I know
I'll never look good in.

On the Gurney with the Village People

The anesthesiologist
walks over to my hospital bed smiling:
'*Well, we had fun,*' she laughs,
meaning the operating room staff
who played both sides of the Disco tape
I brought in for my outpatient surgery.

Side two as I remember has 'YMCA"
the big 1970's hit by the Village People.
I hope it was playing
when Dr. Hall leaned over my body
to cut out the tumor
that shouldn't have been there.

Now I'm wondering if the young technician
hummed to herself
over the instrument table, or
if the scrub nurse
tapped her foot, even a little,
as she reached under the metal shelf
for another clean towel.

Sedation leaves the mind a blank,
not unlike those blanks I get
trying to remember
the names of the sweaty young men
I danced with years ago,
their gorgeous white suits still shining
somewhere with my strappy high heels
and silver tube top.

The disco floor has been
replaced by the recovery room.
but I'm not complaining – not really –
these songs make me smile,
singin' those same four letters over and over.

Recovery

The anesthesia still rolled in
across my body this morning
like one of those unexpectedly strong waves
that quickly pulls you
under the water.

It's Wednesday, around noon,
the day after my surgery.
My body is a village on a coastline
where the residents are
standing on their front porches,
waiting for the sky to clear.

I'm sitting up in bed
with my tapes and a few books,
the windows wide open
so a cheerful sun
can lower itself down
onto the peace lily,
its long green leaves reaching upward.

I've temporarily left the outside world
for the world of the body:
the chapel of the throat,
blessing itself with green tea and Gatorade;
the shining kingdom of the skull, the brain,
which is trying to decide
where my mother and I
will have dinner Saturday night.

I've the wonderful small towns of
the legs and the feet,
moving a bit more steadily
down this beach,
the whole body (mine!)
stretching itself out
on the red striped towel,
and – very slowly now, very gently,
closing its eyes.

Night Prayers

1.

I'm pretending tonight's no
different than any other night:

the steady hum of passing cars,
Degas, curled into a solid sleep on the sofa.

The fact is tomorrow morning I go
to the hospital again for my second

surgery in eighteen days.
All my friends are saying prayers:

Lucy, kneeling, at the Basilica's
quiet five o'clock mass,

David, walking out of the metro,
waiting to cross Connecticut Avenue,

Jim, at the round kitchen table,
pouring a second cup of coffee,

Retta and Carol at church,
Lexi, on the beach in Santa Cruz,

Wendy, home finally, after a double shift,
and Sherry, watching students drift down the hall,
Melissa, leaning against the piano,
Lori, writing a card at her desk downstairs,

Keith, putting the scripts away,
the green clock glowing from the desk,

Marcia, on her cell phone,
driving home before it begins to rain.

2.

Here is Degas again, hind legs against the cushion.
I know I need to get to bed.
I hesitate before I switch off the light,

imagining prayers drifting down around me,
falling steadily one
after the other,

all night long while I sleep,
while Degas sleeps,
while Degas and I sleep.

Section Two

First Day of Gorgeous Weather

Brownies

I want to ask the young woman
in the light pink leotard
seated next to me in this café
if the dark hand of breast cancer
has ever touched her,
while she's paying her bill
and gathering her things,
as Lori and I decide
on the brownies and ice cream.

When the two large white bowls
arrive at our table today,
a week after my surgery,
on the first day of gorgeous weather,
on the first day I've been out,
I know I'll finish
the brownies
and the vanilla ice cream too,
the thin line of syrup
pooling a bit
in the bottom of the bowl.

The syrup's sticky on the spoon
but that's ok —
it's sweet, harmless,
unless I count the calories,
which I'll do some other time,
but not while Lori and I
are eating the most popular item here,
the two of us talking and laughing
in front of this window,

where the cherry trees are blooming
all around the park,
and the only thing I feel
that's touching me now
is sun, only the sun.

Her Treatment Begins

First, I would tell you:
you do not need to be afraid.
The treatment room is not large.
It is completely white except
for a wide green border by the ceiling,
like the color of the sea in late September.
Think of fish swimming there.
An assistant with a colored pen
will draw marks along your breast.
Think of diving, high tide,
drying your hair on the back porch in the sun.
Across the room from you is a laser beam.
Throughout the treatment, the beam stays on.
Remember how you rode your bike
barefoot around the lagoon,
how the six o'clock siren made the dogs bark.

You must lie still, arms
raised and crossed over your head.
There will be a noise, steady and loud.
Remember music in the evening drifting
out the dining room windows.
Then the treatment is over.
You can get dressed and go home.
Sleep tonight on your good side.
Ask this generous world
to fold its great wings
over you and let you rest.

Shine the Light on Me

The red laser
in this treatment room
reminds me of the *Midnight Special*,

the freight train convicts
watched for at night
from their darkened cells.

If the engine light shone
on them through the bars,
they'd be set free.

I'm on a table in a clinic,
not some dead dog jail cell.
I've never murdered anyone.

The only law broken here
is the body's law:
that its millions of cells

will replicate flawlessly.
Now some imperfect ones
have slipped under the fence.

I watch as the laser
kills each renegade cell,
a cold war with my name on it.

In a few weeks
I'll walk out this front door,
spared from my own death,

no more high pitch of the laser.
Instead, the long low rumble
of the *Midnight Special*

roaring past me,
huge light shining,
as I turn and head for home.

The Woman Who Lived

Someone in my support group today
mentioned a member who'd died,
how, *she hadn't taken
care of herself.*

Now I'm thinking about her,
wondering what she did
during that last year
before the final darkness.

Did she start smoking again?
Stay up all night
dancing at the late night clubs,
weave home along some state highway?

Maybe she threw out her vitamins,
ate whatever she felt like,
skipped mammograms, even though
I assume she knew better.

I wonder, at the end,
if her hair had grown back,
or if she'd made any plans
for who would take the cat.

When I came home,
I started dinner, then sat
at my desk, switched on
the big light.

What would she say if
she saw me writing down
words for her to hear,
she who won't be in the room

on the first floor of the hospital
where five women meet monthly
going on as best they can,
still saying how they miss her.

"C"

See me
without a bra,
you won't miss this scar

like one of those big capitol C's
I drew back in grade school:

C, C, C, C
all across the lined paper
until I did it perfectly.

Even now,
months after my surgery,
when I feel tired or bored,

I take a piece of paper
and write out letters,
X's, Y's, M's –

I think I still do them well,

except for this C shaped scar
   that's carved in my body

like a new language
   I need to take,
   or
   an unfamiliar letter
      I have to write.

I take my good pen
and do the best I know how.

Then I leave it alone,
   just as it is,

and go on
   to the rest of the letters.

Solids

Look at all the solids you bought
Lucy said

when I showed her my new clothes:
solid separates,
off- white, black, apricot.

Before the surgeries, I used to wear
stripes with circles,
checks with spangles,
prints with flower patterns –

a mishmash of styles running
in every direction.

A life- threatening illness changes people,
Lucy told me.

I think it's true. I like
feeling into my closet

for a peach colored jacket,
no dingy stripes to confuse me.

I'm a survivor now.
I want to walk into the world,

and look like I know where I'm going,
both feet hitting the ground,

sturdy, steady, *solid*.

Biafine

(for E.F.)

My cousin needs something
for her skin, red and itchy now
following weeks of radiation
after breast cancer.
The Aloe Vera she uses is ok, but –
did I know something better?

Biafine - I spelled it out for her -
the creme lotion I used to
smooth over my own breast
to stop the burning,
and bring the heat down,
white mountain cool again
like the color of the box
it came in.

My cousin's been crying a lot.
Her body's doing its best
to whoosh away the fears.
I try to tell her how
she's making progress,
that change is almost always slow,

and healing starts small,
sometimes no more than
a thin circle of lotion
to cool everything down,
and then going from there,
and then going from there.

Restoration

Paul, the plumber, comes today
to fix what's broken:
my john that won't flush,
the stopped up sink,
the worn out cold water valve
in the shower.

I watch him walk in the door
carrying his metal tool box.
I hear him sigh as he runs
back downstairs
to get a new piece of pipe
out of his truck.

Now he's back in the bathroom,
whack, whack, clang.
I like looking at that shiny new pipe
knowing whatever's damaged
can be repaired.

Later today
I go to my last radiation treatment.
Over the next few weeks
my body will repair itself,
slowly, cell by cell.

Afterwards I'll come home again
to hot and cold water:

Do you have happy pipes? my mother
    asks when she calls.

Yes, I tell her.
    The water's flowing, I think everything's ok.

Women Inventors

In 1971, after her surgery,
my mother folded a washcloth
in half and stuffed it
inside her bra,
a temporary solution,
a kind of clumsy swaddling
to hide her body's wound.

After my diagnosis,
she told me about the washcloth.
How she stood and saw herself
for the first time in the bathroom mirror
with its un-kind colorless globes...

Now I watch myself follow
in her lineage,
snipping a large white sponge
in two, or
cutting cushion foam
from the underside
of my rattan sofa.

Like my mother, I conduct
experiments of my own,
jotting down notes for women
who'll come after me,
inventors, too,
taking whatever the world offers:

cotton, fiber, foam,
re-inventing the body
we all began with,
this yielding compound
of blood and nerve and bone.

After Breast Cancer

My doctor's appointments used to be routine:
yearly blood test,
occasional cortisone shot for my bad foot,

pulled back muscle,
winter cough from the dry air or,
a dark mole removed from my shoulder.

But since last spring,
a doctor's appointment in my daybook
keeps me turning past readings & rehearsals

to that one page,
a door into my doubts
the next one weeks away

before a surgeon or oncologist
will be standing over me,
examining my treatment site

checking the ecosystem of my body:
cells, lymph nodes, tissues,
searching for what shouldn't be there.

Every few months I'll go back,
an invisible tether yoking me
to my new watchful doctors,

to the same lavender bruise where
they draw the blood,
to blood pressure higher than I want,

wishing these new routines
were like cleaning off my desk, or
lugging the trash downstairs,

the mind humming its little tune,
ambling along as always
into the clean start of another day.

A Good Report

is what I'm looking for
in this follow-up appointment

today with Dr. Fowler.
He'll look carefully at my skin,

better now, a few weeks after
the radiation

the area around my scar
still raised, but less sore.

He'll ask me:
Have you have gone back to the gym?
Are you still writing?

He's a practical man,
He knows I need something

I can take with me – a lab report, a statistic,
a summary: *everything looks good*.

I'll tuck the report in my folder,
something to hold onto

as I walk out through the waiting room
where the radio's playing Whitney Houston,

and the leafy green plants in the wicker baskets
are doing just fine, no matter the season.

Section Three

Living in the Spring

Blue Bike

I went back to the health club today
and signed up for strength training

with a muscular young woman
in a high blonde ponytail
and black sweat pants.

She took notes as we talked,
asking questions now and then
about my recent course of radiation.

Another survivor I trained, she said,
*just made a 50 mile bike ride
across the state of Vermont.*

I pictured a woman about my own age
in white shorts and a helmet
tearing past a dark pine forest

bits of gravel spraying up
from under the wheels
of her bright blue bike.

I sat back on the sofa
feeling something deeper
than the muscles I'd be training soon,

knowing she and I
pulled through the same exercises
and look at her now:

cheering with the crowd
as a friend from home
points a camera

and captures her:
Go girl go!
sailing over that finish line.

Guide Book

Too bad there isn't a guide book
for women like me

ready to date again
after surgery,

some kind of brochure that tells
you how to lean forward in your seat

at a restaurant
without pulling the skin over your scar,

how to react
when the lacy new bra you bought

looks great on the right,
awful on the left,

or how to really pace yourself
when taking off your clothes,

the three inch scar on your breast
ticking like a time bomb – well,

maybe he'll have a scar too.
Both of you mortal human beings,

flesh divided by flesh
and sewn back up again,

into life, into laughter,
when it starts pouring outside

and you're hand in hand
sprinting for the car,

with no time to even *think*
about a guide book,

and much too busy by then
to try to write one.

Poem

A friend from Philadelphia called today
with news that a woman poet he knew
had died of breast cancer.

She'd kept her illness a secret
from everyone except
a small circle of close friends.

I met her only once, at a poetry reading.
She introduced all the readers,
then sat down quietly in the front row
for the next two hours to listen.

Now I wonder if I were to walk into her house,
whether I'd find one of her poems

vital, lovely, a key,

even if all its transitions
weren't perfectly clear yet,

or if the initial form weren't
quite right,

even if the lyric moment,
right at the end,

was left open –
as though waiting for more music

Jupiter

According to my horoscope,
Jupiter enters my sign next month:

opportunity, good will,
good fortune, good vibes, good shoes,

Maybe it'll cancel out
all the bad luck
or whatever it is

that happened to me last spring:
biopsy, surgery, radiation.

I've never thought of myself as lucky,
even though I have a rabbit's foot
at home and even some crystals –

But this week it's clear
certain planetary bodies are moving
themselves into alignment.

If I could look up at Jupiter,
maybe my luck will change:

no more symptoms or surgery,
no recurrence two years from now.

If what they say is true
about Jupiter, that
big, bright planet is luck.

Too big for my charm bracelet,
of course, but not for my life.

Blossoms

Debbie, herself a survivor,
wished me happy anniversary March 27th,
a year ago today when
I was wheeled into surgery
and came out changed and alive.

Now I'm watching
the enormous magnolia tree
blooming in Marianne's front yard,
hundreds of pink colored petals;
they'd be gone in a few days
after a hard rain, or too strong a wind.

I think about the women
who aren't here to see them,
women without an anniversary,
that marker that says: *go on, go on.*

A late afternoon sun climbs
through the tree's uppermost branches
almost dizzy with all that pink.

As I watch the petals lifting – my eyes
moving from blossom to blossom -
I think about that word, *anniversary,*
celebration, of course, and *going on,*
and also: *remembering.*
Also: pink. This pink.

September Morning

I have the phone against my ear,
trying to schedule a mammogram.
Sorry, the clerk's saying,
We're doubled booked. I listen,
wanting the tightness in my stomach
to disappear, hoping that I won't
have to keep saying, *cancer.*
I need to get off the phone,
let the call dissolve itself

into nothing, that receding.
I grab my keys and my sunglasses
and head down the street,
more than a statistic, or another case,
or a file with a notation,
just a woman walking
in a hurry to the coffee shop
hoping the cinnamon rolls
won't be all gone
by the time she gets there.
I've time, I've time.

Years Out

is a phrase you hear
survivors say:

I'm three years out,
or seven years out,

counting the time between
diagnosis and now,

with no new sign of cancer,
no small sudden lump in the breast.

Now I'm crossing the months
off my own calendar

cutting them into confetti
which one night

three years, seven years from now,
I'll stand outside

and fling as far as I can
into all those shining stars

a million light years away.

Lifeboats

Enhancers are what the sales lady
called the light foam pads
she carried into the dressing room
along with my new bra's.
I could have paddled off the *Titanic*
with these boys,

instead of trying to stuff
them into my bra,
imagining one shooting out
the first time I try to lift
a heavy bag of groceries.

Or when I dash to the ladies room
in the middle of a meal so
I can re-assemble
the part of my chest
that's plopped out
onto the salmon.

Later I described them to Lucy:

Don't you wear them,
you'll look like Madonna
in those bullet bras from the 8O's.

She's right.
I'm trying to be patient,
extra kind to myself
in front of the mirror,
examining my body's change -
a *sea change*, I say,
give me a friend,
a fashion device, anything –
so I won't go under.

Going Easy

I can't get rid of the extra weight
around my waist now
since I started Tamoxifen,
the pill that's supposed to keep
the cancer from coming back.

I can't buy clothes the way
I used to – when my waist
easily wore a size eight,
wide leather wrap belts,
around snazzy palazzo pants.

On my bad days
when I step off the scale
again, faintly annoyed,
I know I can spent the rest of the day
upset and restless,

wanting to look like someone
I'm not anymore,
instead of the way I am,
in a new pair of slacks,
bigger than I'm used to buying,

light soft silk
slightly flared,
not perfect of course,
but well fitting, comfortable,
easy to wear,
hard to herd in my closet.

Party, April 2004

You might think I'm crazy
planning now
for a party next April

a year since my surgery,
but I already have the theme:
Living in the Spring --

What do you think?
Jim could decorate the front hall
white tulle, ribbons,

big bunches of pink peonies
if they're out by then.
I wonder if I could get Degas

to wear a bow?
I think I'll play Verdi
for the first arrivals

and later on, when Thomas comes,
we'll have Cher and Disco
so people can dance.

Or Lori and I could sing:
　　I Could Have Danced All Night, or My Blue Heaven.
　　　　When it gets dark

we'll turn on the hall Christmas lights
　　and the candles in the bay window,
　　　　everyone will still be milling around

Marne's old steamer trunk,
　　laughing, and talking – happy, content.
　　　　Do you know what I'm saying?

I'll be alive, actually *living,*
　　there'll be lights and music,
　　　　nobody will want to say goodnight

and go home.
　　So if you call, wondering
　　　　if it's too late to stop by,

I'll say *no, no,*
　　come on over
　　　　we're still here,

We're still here.

photo: L. Neikirk

About the Author

Sandra Evans Falconer is a 1999 recipient of an Individual Artists Award in Poetry from The Maryland State Arts Council. She is the author of two poetry chapbooks, *Absent Sisters*, and *Imagining the World*. Her poems have appeared in numerous regional publications, and have also been set to music and adapted for the stage. Sandra holds graduate degrees in social work and dramatic arts, and also an MFA in Creative Writing from Spalding University in Louisville, Kentucky. In addition to her writing life, Sandra is also a dancer and performer, and the founder of *Spirit Bound*, a therapeutic dance program for the health-care community. Sandra lives in Baltimore, Maryland, where she works for the University of Maryland Medical Center. Her next book project is *The Lucky Spot Dance,* a collection of poems about her late brother, Steven, which she hopes to have adapted to the stage and to film. Sandra is also working on a series of poetic monologues about the *RMS Titanic*.

As of March 2009,
Sandra Evans Falconer
has been cancer free
for 6 years.